SUCCESSFUL NEGOTIATION

Tips to negotiate effectively and get real results

Written by Florence Schandeler

Translated by Carly Probert

HOW TO NEGOTIATE SUCCESSFULLY   1

SMOOTH NEGOTIATING: THE BASICS   3

Apprehending the negotiation

Types of negotiations and relational games

Preparation

Negotiating to a written agreement

TOP TIPS   19

FAQS   22

What arguments can I use in favour of negotiation?

What rules must be followed for the discussion to be constructive?

How do I know if the exchange has been successful?

How can I negotiate without seeming manipulative?

The other party seems closed to all my attempts to compromise, what should I do?

What are the characteristics of a good negotiator?

OVER TO YOU   27

Establishing an agenda for the negotiation

Personal preparation for the negotiation

FURTHER READING   30

HOW TO NEGOTIATE SUCCESSFULLY

- **Problem:** How can I defend my interests while taking into account those of the other party, in order to reach a satisfactory, sustainable and strong compromise?
- **Uses:** In both personal and professional contexts, knowing how to carry out a negotiation to solve a conflict, to conclude agreements centred on the interests of both parties and to strengthen interpersonal relationships with your interlocutors.
- **Context:** Professional relationships, communication, argumentation, conflict management, etc.
- **FAQs:**
  - What arguments can I use in favour of negotiation?
  - What rules must be followed for the discussion to be constructive?
  - How do I know if the exchange has been successful?
  - How can I negotiate without seeming manipulative?
  - The other party seems closed to all my attempts at compromise, what should I do?
  - What are the characteristics of a good negotiator?

Tired of a society with unilateral and hierarchical power, the mentality of the past thirty years has evolved into a growing interest in the principles of negotiation and cooperation. The law of the strongest is now over: to ensure efficient work and positive energy, we must work together, create together and co-write the rules and projects that mark our daily lives. This trend is evident in both the professional sector and in our private lives.

Indeed, we negotiate every day: where to spend the next Christmas holidays, what film to see at the cinema, to get a raise, for more flexible hours, to finalise a contract that is favourable to both parties, etc. Therefore, learning to express our views and defending them while respecting those of the other party is crucial to leaving a negotiation feeling satisfied and confident.

Negotiating means daring to say what you want and raising points of contention in order to improve our daily or professional lives. It also means setting goals and leeway for reaching them. Finally, it means attempting to measure risks and compare them with the benefits of making changes. In 50 minutes, this book will help you to discover the challenges of this approach and the strategies you should implement for successful future negotiations.

SMOOTH NEGOTIATING: THE BASICS

APPREHENDING THE NEGOTIATION

Constitutive elements

Negotiations consist of two elements that define and distinguish them from any other communicative actions:

- an opponent
- a common goal.

A negotiation pits two people or two parties with conflicting interests on one or more points against each other, face to face. Unlike a mere discussion or a pointless argument, the parties, driven by a common interest to come to an agreement, gather around a table to find common ground.

The argumentative exchange that takes place during a negotiation is therefore more complex and richer than that of a dispute in which the participants are content to shout their opinions and line up arguments without even listening to the other party. Through their desire to find an agreement, the negotiators need to be attentive to the needs and requests of the other party. Without neglecting their own interests, they should consider a solution that satisfies both parties. This is where the difficulty of the task lies.

When and why should I negotiate?

In order to improve our lives, we all have to negotiate both in our daily and our professional lives. Several objectives can lead to this approach:

- Resolving conflict (e.g. to develop a better division of household tasks between family members);
- Amending a contract (e.g. negotiating a salary increase or switching to part-time work);
- Improving an offer (e.g. as part of a property sale, the seller and the buyer must agree on a price);
- Finalising an agreement to optimise collaboration (e.g. a sports team and its main sponsor negotiate the money allocated, depending on the placement and the size of the logo on the players' shirts).

Each party has something to gain from negotiation, so rather than sticking to your guns, you must engage in the process with a harmonious approach. However, before starting, you should check that the process is worth it. If, for example, you want to negotiate a schedule change when your employer has already modified it in your favour, you run the risk of your new request being interpreted as eternal dissatisfaction or as a sign of arrogance. This may make him overlook any of your future demands.

Overcoming prejudices

In our relationships, we act based on our previous experiences and preconceptions. Therefore, for the negotiation to go well, we must first condition ourselves to perceive the positive image of the process, far from stereotypes and prejudices that overpower our understanding.

Negotiation	NOT Negotiation
<ul><li>Being part of a group decision</li><li>Listening</li><li>Treating everyone with respect</li><li>Finding common ground where everyone feels the benefits</li><li>Building relationships of trust and collaboration between the different participants</li></ul>	<ul><li>Submitting to the decisions of others</li><li>Being influenced</li><li>Using force, blackmail or lies to impose your point of view</li><li>Being stubborn, thinking that giving in to a compromise means failing</li></ul>

TYPES OF NEGOTIATIONS AND RELATIONAL GAMES

'Principled negotiation'

There are different types of negotiations. Roger Fisher (1922-2012) and William Ury (born in 1953), founders of the Harvard National Project and negotiation specialists, have developed the method of principled negotiation, or win-win negotiation.

> "The method of principled negotiation developed at the Harvard Negotiation Project is to decide issues on their merits rather than through a haggling process focused on what each side says it will and won't do. It suggests that you look for mutual gains wherever possible, and that where your interests conflict, you should insist that the result be based on some fair standards independent of the will of either side."
> (Fisher and Ury, 1985: 6)

Principled negotiation consists of four principles:

- The dispute should be treated separately from the people involved (who have a role to play and must ensure they stick to a side in the debate);
- The discussion should focus on the interests of both parties and not their positions;
- It is better to imagine a large sample of potential solutions, rather than stay fixed on one;
- All participants must require the result to be based on objective and assessable criteria. These will be listed as "The decision will be respected when…".

Compliance with these four criteria ensures that we stay within the framework of a rational discussion, which covers only the subject of the debate and not people's reputations, thus finding a practical and beneficial solution for both parties. This approach has the advantage of preventing the participants from taking a position they would struggle to leave, for fear of having to admit a semi-failure or feeling that they have lost face. The negotiation has a greater chance of success by starting from what is possible to submit for both parties and seeking common interests, rather than highlighting points of contention.

This technique is ideal for obtaining a satisfactory result for both parties because it does not mean fully satisfying the claims of both sides (this would be impossible), but rather reaching a fair agreement after a respectful discussion. The two specialists oppose the method of distributive (or competitive) bargaining, in which each party tries to maximise their gains without regard for the needs of the other. It is either win-win or lose-lose if negotiations fail.

We can illustrate this type of negotiation with an example: an employee (E) has worked at the same bank in contact centre service for several years. His manager (M) is very happy with his work and considers him to be one of the most efficient staff members in the department. However, the employee does not feel fulfilled by his work and would like to work somewhere we he has more direct and personalised contact with customers. His manager does not immediately see the benefit of satisfying his request: the experience of his employee makes him very competent. By changing his position, he will need to find someone just as qualified as him as a replacement: for him, it is a financial investment. However, if the manager refuses to budge, he has more to lose by accepting the request of his colleague, as shown in the diagram below. By applying principled negotiation and taking into account the objectives of each party, the discussion is more likely to lead to a solution that is acceptable to both.

GOOD TO KNOW

Whatever the subject of the debate, keep in mind that any speaker, regardless of their culture or party in the debate, will act in order to protect their basic needs, namely:

- A desire for security;
- The wish to live in economic wellbeing;
- The importance of belonging to a community (professional body, position within the company, family, etc.);
- The need to feel free and be the master of his own choices.

Cooperation or ratio of power?

As it aims to initiate a common and mutual understanding, principled negotiation is, by definition, cooperative. It invites parties to listen and understand everything in order to find a solution that is suitable for all.

However, as in all human relationships, the relationships between the parties may be asymmetric, and this introduces a ratio of power into the equation. According to Lionel Bellenger (company management specialist, born in 1947), there are six types of pre-determining factor that determine the links between participants during a negotiation:

- hierarchical (rank difference within the company)
- number (when one solution satisfies the highest number of people)
- temporary (preponderance of a company on the market)
- arising from competence (presence of an expert on the subject to be negotiated or someone with more experience)
- natural (facing a charismatic personality)
- cultural (the authority of elders in certain areas).

Given all these factors, it seems clear that the relationship between the negotiators is rarely neutral. It is therefore necessary to analyse and consider this power struggle, which partly determines the course of the conversation. If the latter is highly unbalanced, the agreement will naturally converge towards the wishes of the superior party. However, keep in mind that if a negotiation has been set up, it is to find benefits for all, and that a conversation based solely on power ratios can only engender conflict. Negotiation, even with the imbalance of forces, is intended to find a creative and collaborative solution, allowing everyone to find their place and be involved in decisions.

Thus, subject to the authority of his parents, a teenager will respond more readily to doing housework if he can negotiate some free time on Friday evening, instead of feeling unjustly imprisoned in the family home. Similarly, an employee will be more involved in his job if he can make a contribution to building projects and the company's organization, instead of being limited to all the rules of his contract.

THE REQUIREMENTS OF NEGOTIATION

Negotiating means accepting that a third party is involved in making a decision that affects us. Therefore, in order for the negotiation to be constructive and fulfilling for everyone, the following must be accepted:

- not having full control of the situation;
- enduring some tension, caused by disagreement that is proportional to the divergence of interests;
- having to defend own interests to another party;
- not always achieving the goals we had set;
- complying with a number of rules so that the discussion is honest and respects all views and interests.

Negotiator profiles

In a group discussion, we adopt roles based on our character and our involvement in the debate. Each negotiator acts according to their personality, strengths and weaknesses, and, depending on the components and circumstances, operates with a certain dynamic.

With these variables, each participant will adopt, consciously or not, one or more positions in the debate. In his book, *The Fundamentals of Negotiation*, Lionel Bellenger highlights ten types of roles:

- **The leader**, who takes the lead in the conversation. They are followed by the group and speak on their behalf;
- **The regulator**, who is the team leader of the group. They distribute speaking time and reformulate proposals in order to mark progress in the discussion;
- **The follower**, who follows the general movement and approves the decisions of the group;
- **The rebel**, who denies and argues against the ideas of the group, putting the main objective at risk;
- **The law-enforcer** who takes the role of policeman. They recall the rules and ensure that the agenda is respected;
- **The expert**, with experience or expertise who acts as an authority on the issue to be negotiated;
- **The naïve person**, i.e. the seemingly innocent one, who questions to clarify the views expressed by the group;
- **The orchestrator**, who continues searching for a compromise. Their purpose is to preserve the peace in the group, at the risk of offering complex solutions to satisfy all participants;

- **The producer**, active and positive in the collaboration. They offer ideas without imposing them;
- **The obstructionist**, set on disrupting the group, preventing progress and tending to discourage everyone.

By observing the positions adopted within the group, we realise that a collective decision is both facilitated by certain attitudes and tested by others. In this context, the success of the negotiations depends on the strength of the group leaders and the ability of all participants to identify the objective and want to reach it.

PREPARATION

Preparing for a negotiation is an essential step: arriving with your hands in your pockets and your confidence as your only weapon is the best way to fail! This step will help you to define the subject of the negotiation and the challenges that underpin communication, as well as to develop a strategy to achieve your goals.

Diagnostic

The diagnostic phase is essential and necessary for any negotiation. You must study the subject of the negotiation and the situation and learn about the various parties and the interests they will defend to you during the debate. For this, inform yourself on the strengths and weaknesses of the opposing party, as well as their needs and their goals. Also investigate what the competition is offering in order to adapt. All of this information will be an asset to your argument.

Objectives

Once the basis has been established, after defining what you will discuss and with whom, you have to look at your own goals and how to achieve them. If you start a negotiation without knowing what you want, you will leave empty-handed.

This is where you determine your wiggle room and your "BA" (Best Alternative). To measure your leeway, or "zone of possible agreement" (ZPA), analyse the situation by asking yourself the following questions: "What can I claim? What can I gain from this exchange?". Make your best estimate (best-case scenario), i.e. an unexpected victory, and your lowest estimate, which represents the lowest acceptable gain that is "always better than nothing". The gap between the two is your ZPA. Give precise evidence, for example using numbers, particularly in the case of an application for a promotion.

In the event that the other party will concede nothing, be prepared to reject their proposals. For your breaking point, where you must present your refusal, determine your BATNA (Best Alternative to a Negotiated Agreement). This is defined by Fisher and Ury (in their book *Getting to Yes*) as the best alternative outside of negotiating.

Take the example of two employees who ask to switch teams. The first wants to switch because of tensions that he has to manage daily and which are disagreeable to him; the second wants to switch because he can no longer bear to work with his colleagues who harass him, and he may burn out if the situation persists. For the first employee, the BATNA is to stay in the team, since he can put up with it. For the second, the BATNA would be to remove the team member who is the most negative.

The definition of BATNA is therefore inherent in the analysis of each situation: what are we willing to accept, or what can we accommodate in a given context? Finally, if no solution is found at the end of the exchange, you can make a withdrawal hypothesis and propose to resume the discussion after a time of reflection for both parties, or a new item for discussion.

Best case scenario (BCS)	Best outcome (often unrealistic). Trying to bluff to maximise gains.
Risk of refusal	
Good outcome	Hoped-for offer or upper limit (realistic).
Acceptable outcome	Aim: avoiding the lowest estimate – managing the margin based on the good outcome.
Lowest estimate	Reserve or lowest offer.
Refusal line – BATNA	
Withdrawal outcome	Failure of the negotiation – stop the negotiation and take time to reflect or examine another element.

Logistics

If you are taking care of the organisation of the debate, make sure you have invited all the participants and have:

- A precise and appropriate location (so that it is possible to be isolated and quiet);
- Arrangements for the occasion (necessary equipment and seating arrangement of all participants around the table);
- A set schedule (start time and time allocated to the debate).

NEGOTIATING TO A WRITTEN AGREEMENT

Good attitudes

The driving force behind the action for all participants is, of course, the desire to reach an agreement, which is the main objective of the negotiations. Therefore, everyone must act along two main lines during the negotiation:

- Asserting their position in the discussion by explaining their interests and arguing to justify their views;
- Listening to the other party by not challenging them or immediately judging their arguments. Try to imagine yourself in their shoes to prevent you from having a projective attitude (where we assimilate our own interests with the common interests) and thus understand and accept differences of opinion.

As you prepare for the idea of compromise or consensus, focusing on the interest that would lead to a successful negotiation, you will manage to channel your actions towards the essential points of the debate and merge your interests with those of the other party. For constructive negotiations, adopt the following attitudes:

- Establish the relationship before the negotiation. To do this, maintain an initial speaking time so that everyone can freely express their views without trial and without feeling disputed or contradicted;
- Show signs of acceptance and recognition when others are speaking;
- Encourage the other party to concretely define their expectations. Do not hesitate to ask for clarification if you do not understand;
- Analyse and measure the risks and consequences of your decisions for each party;
- At the end of the exchange, assess the failures and suc-

cesses and highlight what worked, what was positive and what was negative in the exchange.

Possible outcomes

After the group discussion, we can achieve four different results, which must be considered before starting a negotiation and which will have to be followed up.

- In the first case, the negotiation will fail and the discussion will end in **disagreement**. This can be seen as:
  - Objective, if the negotiators agree on the fact that they cannot agree;
  - Confrontational, when negotiations go wrong (personal attacks, humiliation of a speaker);
  - Delayed, when the players decide to postpone decisions.
- Secondly, negotiations may lead to **concessions**. This means that one of the two parties involved has conceded on a point without getting any compensation. In this case, we are faced with a scenario where there is a winner and a loser.
- **Compromise** forms a third possibility. The two sides

both make concessions to reach an agreement where the essential interests of each are guaranteed.

- Last scenario: negotiation is a total success and the solution found together unanimously suits all players. Here we have reached a **consensus**.

After an agreement has been reached at the end of the negotiation, all is not over. It is now necessary to verify that it will be respected by all parties. To do this, it is useful to write down the implications of this agreement (by answering the questions in the table below) and provide a copy to all signatories so that they are aware of the measures and steps needed to keep their word.

Who? Which people are involved in the agreement?	
What? What does the agreement entail, in concrete terms (in terms of changes in behaviour or actions to complete)?	
Where? When? Where and in what context does the agreement apply?	
How? What indicators show that the agreement has been respected?	

TOP TIPS

- **Dare to assert yourself.** Confidence in your strengths and motivations is an important factor for a successful negotiation. To ready yourself to defend your position in the debate, prepare, preferably in writing – to better define the ins and outs of your argument – a list of issues, the interests you are defending and underlying arguments. Be convinced by your words to persuade the other party.
- **Ask questions.** Questioning is a tool that allows you to build a conversation and make the reflection more concrete and explicit. In all phases of the negotiation, from preparation up to the final result, ask yourself and the other party questions: "What elements do I want to see change after this exchange? Why? What are my interests and those of the other party who are finalising the agreement? What consequences will this decision have for my work?" It is essential for each party to measure the interests and benefits of the proposals raised during the discussion.
- **Never lose sight of your goal.** The best way to leave a negotiation with nothing is forgetting what you wanted to gain: a tangential discussion is likely to lead you from one subject to another and you could soon become distracted. Don't lose sight of why you are there and always keep your goal in mind. If you are worried about forgetting, write it down. Putting it in front of you will refocus the debate when it starts to deviate from the right path.
- **Locate and explicitly state common interests.** A debate

of dominance where everyone tries to take all the credit and refuses to give in at the risk of losing face is likely to be fruitless. Start with a good foundation by listing the common interests of both parties before nothing the points of differences and needs of each. You are more likely to arrive at a positive result after presenting the benefits of getting along with others.

- **Think of original solutions.** It is possible that at the end of the conversation, no suitable solution will emerge. Therefore, try to open up your field of possibilities by presenting new, innovative and original ideas. They may please your opponent, or allow them to bounce off them.
- **Be an active listener.** Unlike a dispute where everyone stands their ground, a negotiator needs to know how to take into account the views of others. To do this, actively listen to the other party:
  - Encourage discussion with a caring attitude (do not interrupt them while they are speaking, for example);
  - Ask open-ended questions so that they can explain their expectations and needs;
  - Reformulate the arguments that are used to check their understanding.
- These three steps are essential to considering the words of others and avoiding interpreting them with our projective thinking, which reformulates the ideas of others through our own perspective.
- **Keep in mind the importance of kindness among participants.** Negotiation is a collaboration that requires listening and a minimum level of agreement among participants to stimulate the desire to reach a compromise. Therefore, it is obvious that the conversation must

be conducted with care and mutual respect. If a party is depreciated and judged during his contributions, he will not be honest when listing his expectations and interests and will feel aggrieved by the proposed solution. For this reason, they will be reluctant to accept it and will not be interested in respecting the guidelines outlined through the negotiations, thus rendering them useless.

- **Be sure to keep a balance between the two parties.** Negotiation is a process of constructive decision-making that stimulates and enriches the collaboration between colleagues or between two partners. While it is true that during a debate surrounding a disagreement, we can find the scenario of a winner who gets what he wants, faced with a loser who had to make concessions to solve the problem, care must be taken not to multiply and make a habit of this case. A collaboration where concessions are not mutual and where the basic interests of each party are not met, or are constantly challenged, is not destined to last.

- **Take your time and persevere.** There is little chance that your exchange will end in a major success story in just ten minutes. This process requires time and patience. If you want to finish the matter as soon as possible, the other party will have the impression that you are not taking it seriously and will be less inclined to accept an agreement.

- **Ask for more.** If you formulate a single request, it may be refused, while if you express multiple requests, you increase your chance of having at least one accepted.

FAQS

WHAT ARGUMENTS CAN I USE IN FAVOUR OF NEGOTIATION?

We can highlight several benefits:

- It recognises the decision-making powers of everyone and thus empowers the parties involved to reach a decision supported by the group;
- It is part of the learning process in society and in business;
- It spreads values of openness, listening, tolerance and creativity;
- It symbolises democracy and guards against abuses of power;
- It encourages collaboration and helps reinforce links between people;
- When done well, it guarantees quality decision-making through the consideration and confrontation of differing views.

WHAT RULES MUST BE FOLLOWED FOR THE DISCUSSION TO BE CONSTRUCTIVE?

To create a caring and supportive environment for the conversation, follow these tips:

- Ensure that speaking time is allocated fairly. Everyone should have to opportunity to speak freely while being aware of their place in the discussion;
- Take into account the views of others and remain open to

their perspectives, otherwise you will be talking at cross purposes;

- Have a participatory notion of confrontation. Instead of starting the conversation by outlining what everyone is looking for and thus pointing out the differences in opinion, highlight the points of convergence and the common purpose;
- Each participant must explain and demonstrate the merits of his views;
- Watch your body language. Be friendly, welcoming, look the other party in the eye and speak calmly;
- Commit to a collective decision by agreeing to listen to others, answering their questions on your views and changing your opinion to reflect the bigger picture of the debate.

HOW DO I KNOW IF THE EXCHANGE HAS BEEN SUCCESSFUL?

Four concrete questions will allow you to assess if the negotiation has been successful.

	Success	Failure
Did the negotiation allow you to come to a result or agreement (consensus or compromise)?	Yes	No
Did the negotiation answer the concrete interests of both parties and allow them to resolve the conflicts of interests between them?	Yes	No
Did the negotiation compromise the people involved in the decision?	No	Yes
Does the agreement established at the end of negotiation take into account the interests of the community, and is it viable in the long term?	Yes	No

HOW CAN I NEGOTIATE WITHOUT SEEMING MANIPULATIVE?

The fundamental difference between a negotiator and a manipulator is the consideration given to the other party. While a manipulator will act to the detriment of the other party, a negotiator will try to search for solutions that are favourable to both parties.

It is important to keep in mind that we are always interacting with someone who is seeking to receive, not to give. You must therefore ensure, for a sustainable exchange strategy, that the other party is acting in their interests by accepting your proposal.

THE OTHER PARTY SEEMS CLOSED TO ALL MY ATTEMPTS TO COMPROMISE, WHAT SHOULD I DO?

It may be that, even with a strong case, your attempts at compromise prove unsuccessful. The other party will not budge, it is inconceivable for them to accept any of your requests. With such an unequivocal refusal, it is important to understand the reason for their position:

- They cannot agree to your requests for reasons that go beyond their control. In this case, there is no need to urge a person who has no power to give you what you want;
- They may not currently be in a good mood to respond favourably. Overwhelmed by work and stressed by deadlines, this is not the time for them to consider your request. In this case, you can always offer to provide a written report of your request or to talk about it at a more convenient time;
- It could also be that they have no real reason to say no. In this context, try to steer the debate towards the benefits they could derive from an arrangement with you in relation to his current situation.

If the answer is still no, with the aim of understanding your partner and persevering in your application, end the exchange with the questions: "What do you need me to change in order for you to say yes?" and "Under what conditions would you agree to my request?".

WHAT ARE THE CHARACTERISTICS OF A GOOD NEGOTIATOR?

- A good negotiator is well prepared and takes a step back from the situation to be negotiated. As we have already seen, a successful negotiation requires good preparation for the meeting. An effective negotiator will have previously studied the ins and outs of their proposals and will have anticipated the arguments of the other party.
- He respects people, while remaining firm in his objectives. A powerful negotiator can distinguish professional elements from personal elements. For many reasons, it may happen that the negotiation between two colleagues or between and employee and his boss will fail. This does not mean that the relationship between the two people is altered in any way. By setting the boundaries of the debate, and by never casting doubt on the people themselves (by not making any reflection on their character or identity), we can negotiate in a strict and specific manner, and the relationship will be preserved.
- He perceives the other party as a partner. Negotiation is not a boxing match. Ideally, negotiations end with two victories and therefore comprise only winners. In this context, the negotiator should see the other party not as an enemy, but an ally.
- Finally, a good negotiator always takes time, after the exchange, to summarise the positive points of the discussion by recalling that both parties have won in the compromise and highlighting their interest to fulfil their promises. He concludes on a positive note.

OVER TO YOU

ESTABLISHING AN AGENDA FOR THE NEGOTIATION

To help you stay on track during the negotiation, set the topic to be discussed and the objectives of the meeting.

<table>
<tr><td colspan="2">Topic of the negotiation:
....</td></tr>
<tr><td>Date of the meeting:

Time:
Duration:
Place:</td><td>Participants:
•

•

•

•</td></tr>
<tr><td colspan="2">Objective of the negotiation: on what points do we need to agree?
....
....</td></tr>
<tr><td colspan="2">Summary of the decisions agreed by the group (to complete during the meeting):
....
....</td></tr>
</table>

PERSONAL PREPARATION FOR THE NEGOTIATION

Then, to prepare yourself personally, fill in the form below.

<table>
<tr><td colspan="2">Topic of the negotiation:
....</td></tr>
<tr><td colspan="2">My objectives for the negotiation:
....
....
....</td></tr>
<tr><td>Underlying needs of my objectives (why do I need to reach these objectives?):
....
....
....</td><td>My arguments (how will I defend my objectives?):
....
....
....</td></tr>
<tr><td colspan="2">My leeway or zone of possible agreement (ZPA):
• Best case scenario: ....
....
• Good outcome: ....
....
• Acceptable outcome: ....
....</td></tr>
</table>

FURTHER READING

BIBLIOGRAPHY

- Bellenger, L. (2004) *Les fondamentaux de la négociation. Stratégies et tactiques gagnantes*. Paris: ESF éditeur.
- Boutty d'Antin, M., Pluyette, G. and Bensimon, S. (2003) *Art et techniques de la négociation*. Paris: Jurisclasseur.
- Dupont, C. (1990) *La négociation. Conduite, théorie, applications*. Paris: Dalloz.
- Fisher, R. and Ury, W. (1982) *Getting to Yes*. New York: Random House Business Books.
- Moyson, R. (1997) *Communiquer dans l'entreprise et dans la vie. Négociation, collaboration et tolérance*. Brussels : De Boeck University.

www.50minutes.com

Ebook EAN: 9782806279354

Paperback EAN: 9782806284570

Legal Deposit: D/2016/12603/395

Cover: © Primento

Digital conception by Primento, the digital partner of publishers.